Intentionally Left Blank

The *52 Ways For Mom's to Make Money At Home*
book will introduce you to fairly direct and
immediate ways to earn extra income while
you're home.

Whether it's for full-time, part-time or just an
occasional cash infusion, you may find something
here to meet your needs.

Opportunities can be found ranging from
the creative, administrative, technically skilled,
not-so-technically-skilled, and other types of work.

All it takes is a little pluck from you.

To Your Success!

Sincerely,

Jamie J. Jones

Virtual Office Temps

Find a temporary virtual office position. Virtual Office Temps specializes in placing virtual administrative assistants with employers.

Website:
www.virtualassistantjobs.com

Sign Up/Registration Link:
http://www.virtualassistantjobs.com/application.html

Image: Yaron Jeroen van Oostrom /FreeDigitalPhotos.net

GURU

Bid for jobs at Guru.com. This is a bidding website that allows you to bid on jobs. Check out the category titled "Admin" (legal, medical, and accounting support for virtual administrative assistants). You can bid on projects in your area with a free membership or buy a membership which allows you to apply for virtual admin assistant jobs all over the world.

Website:
www.Guru.com

Sign Up/Registration Link:
https://www.guru.com/register_pro.aspx

Technisource

Work as a help desk tech. Technisource is seeking work from home help desk candidates for one of their clients. It is a 24-7 operation so techs should be available for shifts almost anytime.

Website:
www.Technisource.com

Sign Up/Registration Link:
http://www.snip2.com/re/technisource

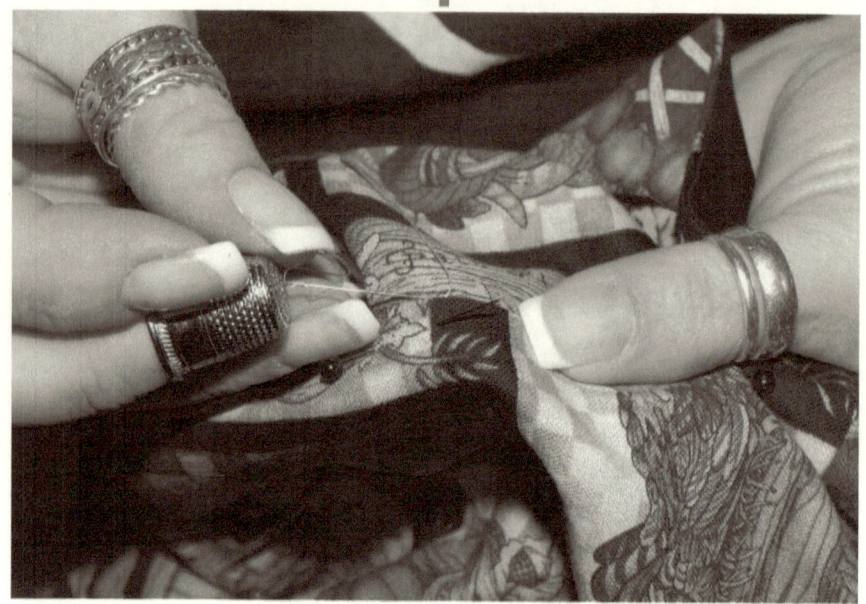

ETSY

Post your handmade products on ETSY.com. Sell crafts, housewares, clothing, accessories, art, needlecraft, and other independent artists.

Website:
www.etsy.com

Sign Up/Registration Link:
https://www.etsy.com/register.php

5

Tutor Agency

Become a tutor for www.TutorAgency.com. They are seeking part-time virtual tutors for all levels including elementary, middle, and high school grades. All tutoring sessions are conducted virtually over the internet via video conference (Skype/WebEx). Compensation is $20.00 an hour and up, based on experience.

Website:
www.TutorAgency.com

Sign Up/Registration Link:
http://www.tutoragency.com/blog1/?page_id=195

Language Line

Use your language skills to work as an interpreter. LanguageLine.com is seeking work at home phone interpreters within the US.

Website:
www.LanguageLine.com

Sign Up/Registration Link:
http://languageline.com/page/interpreter_become/

Brand Institute Inc

Give your opinion and earn money by shaping the future competitive landscape in industries ranging from pharmaceutical to consumer products.

Website:
www.brandinstitute.com

Sign Up/Registration Link:
http://www.snip2.com/re/brandinstitute

Image: Michelle Meiklejohn/FreeDigitalPhotos.net

ELance

Market your skills and talent on the global marketplace and earn money. Elance.com matches buyers and sellers of services that can be easily delivered over the Web, by fax, phone, email or mail.

Website:
www.Elance.com

Sign Up/Registration Link:
http://www.snip2.com/re/elance

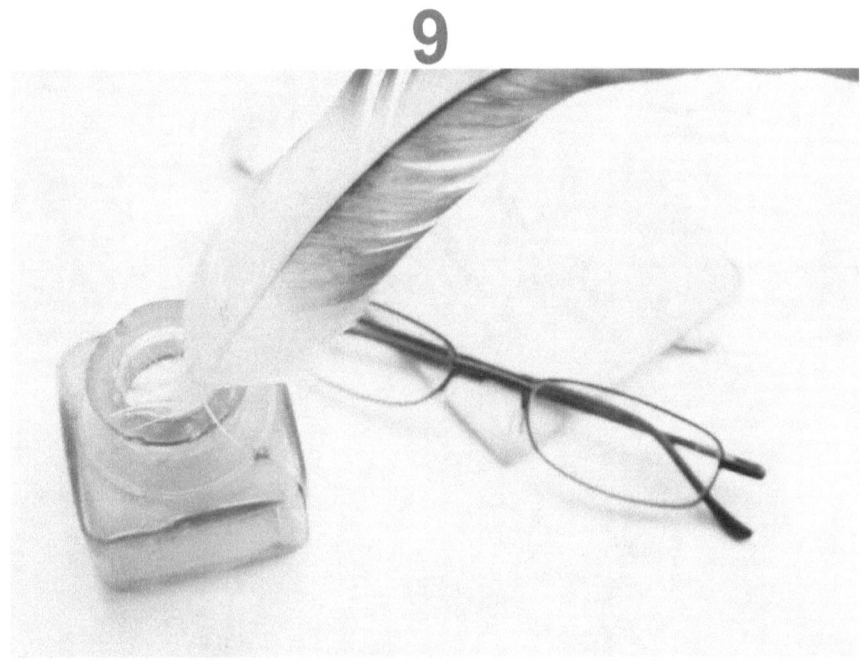

Image: Simon Howden/FreeDigitalPhotos.net

Create Space - Books

Write your book(s), get published, and distribute in one fell swoop. CreateSpace.com is a free online publishing tools and community that can help you complete and sell your work on Amazon.

Website:
www.createspace.com

Sign Up/Registration Link:
https://www.createspace.com/Signup.jsp

Fix Ipods At Home

Repair iPods at home for an income. Learn how to fix iPods for free by visiting ifixit.com *or* methodshop.com. Advertise your services for free on your local craigslist.org site. You can start by offering iPod repair services like microdrive replacement, screen replacement or battery replacement.

Website:
www.ifixit.com *or* www.methodshop.com

Sign Up/Registration Link:
www.ifixit.com/Guide/Browse/iPod *or*

www.method.shop.com/gadgets/ipodsupport/index.shtml

WAHM Job Board

Search the Work at Home Job board at the WAHM site for legitimate virtual administrative assistant and virtual secretary jobs.

Website:
www.wahm.com/jobs.html

Sign Up/Registration Link:
http://www.wahm.com/forum/register.php

Image: Salvatore Vuono/FreeDigitalPhotos.net

Meriwether Publishing Ltd

Channel your inner Shakespeare and receive pay for your talent. Merriwether Publishing pays royalties for your full length plays, musical comedies, oral interpretatons, book adaptations, or books on theatre subjects from anthologies to theatre craft.

Website:
www.meriwetherpublishing.com

Sign Up/Registration Link:
https://www.meriwetherpublishing.com/school.aspx

Image: Maggie Smith/FreeDigitalPhotos.net

Associated Content Inc.

Publish your content on any topic, earn pay for your work. Associated Content Inc. provides a wide range of quality content to readers and publishers by getting them from writers.

Website:
www.associatedcontent.com

Sign Up/Registration Link:
https://publish.associatedcontent.com/signup.shtml

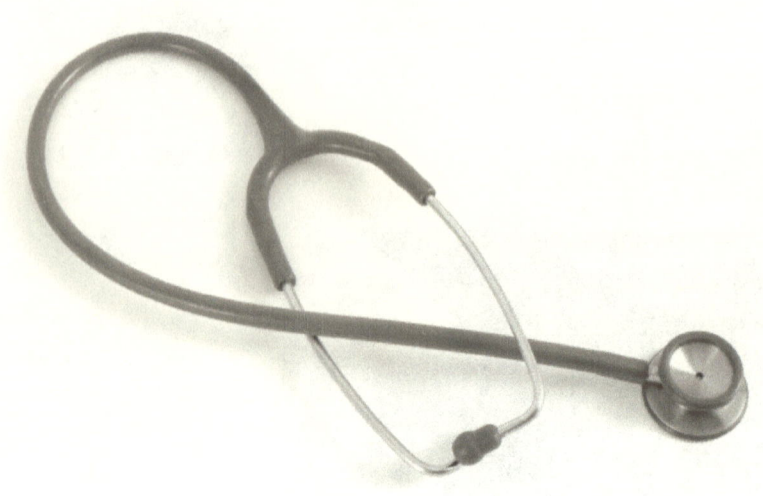

Image: Suat Eman/FreeDigitalPhotos.net

MedQuist

Get hired as a home medical transcriptionist with MedQuist. MedQuist is a leading national provider of medical transcription outsourcing. Applicants must have a high school diploma and at least one year of medical transcription experience.

Website:
www.MedQuist.com

Sign Up/Registration Link:
http://www.snip2.com/re/medquest

Image: FreeDigitalPhotos.net

Educate Online

Work at home as a tutor. Education-Online.com is a
leading provider of online educational instruction
which is delivered live, online, to students who are
struggling in a specific subject or concept.

Website:
www.educate-online.com

Sign Up/Registration Link:
http://www.educate-inc.com/careers/careers.html

Hubpages

Write about what you love and earn cash from it. Hubpages.com provides a place for you to publish your articles. You earn money when the viewers click on the ads on your articles. Earnings are paid to you directly by Google, Amazon and Ebay. Sign up for free.

Website:
www.hubpages.com

Sign Up/Registration Link:
http://hubpages.com/user/new/

Create Space - Music

Compose your music and distribute to fans.
CreateSpace.com is a free online publishing tools
and community that can help you complete and sell
your creative work.
TIP: Check out "100 Tips to Market Your Music" at
www.berkleemusic.com

Website:
www.createspace.com

Sign Up/Registration Link:
https://www.createspace.com/Signup.jsp

Image: Michelle Meiklejohn/FreeDigitalPhotos.net

Squidoo

Write articles or reviews on Squidoo.com to earn some money. Squidoo is the popular publishing platform and community that makes it easy for you to create "lenses" or webpages online. Your earn revenue from referral links to sites like Amazon.com and Ebay.

Website:
www.squidoo.com

Sign Up/Registration Link:
http://www.squidoo.com/member/registration

Digital Point

Create a topic or talking point and participate in the discussion to earn money. DigitalPoint makes money displaying AdSense ads. Once you set up your own AdSense account, 50% of the ad revenue will go to DigitalPoint, the other half is yours.
TIP: Drive traffic to your articles right away – try SubmitExpress.com to send your articles to over 20 major search engines. Do this for each article you write.

Website:
www.DigitalPoint.com

Sign Up/Registration Link:
http://forums.digitalpoint.com/register.php

Software Judge

Give tell-it-like-it-is, no marketing spin, straight talking software reviews for pay. SoftwareJudge.com pays $50 for your review of software programs.

Website:
www.SoftwareJudge.com

Sign Up/Registration Link:
http://www.softwarejudge.com/rules

Need-An-Article.com

Receive regular pay at this pay-per-article site. Need-An-Article.com offers regular paying writing work as well. What many like about them is that they pay weekly on Friday nights.

Website:
www.need-an-article.com

Sign Up/Registration Link:
http://www.needanarticle.com/register/index.php

Image:Andy Newsonn/FreeDigitalPhotos.net

Get Paid for Customer Service

Get paid for your customer service skills. This is an aggregate listing of companies that pay for at home customer service work.

Website:
www.GirlGetPaid.com

Sign Up/Registration Link:
http://girlgetpaid.com/category/customer-service-jobs

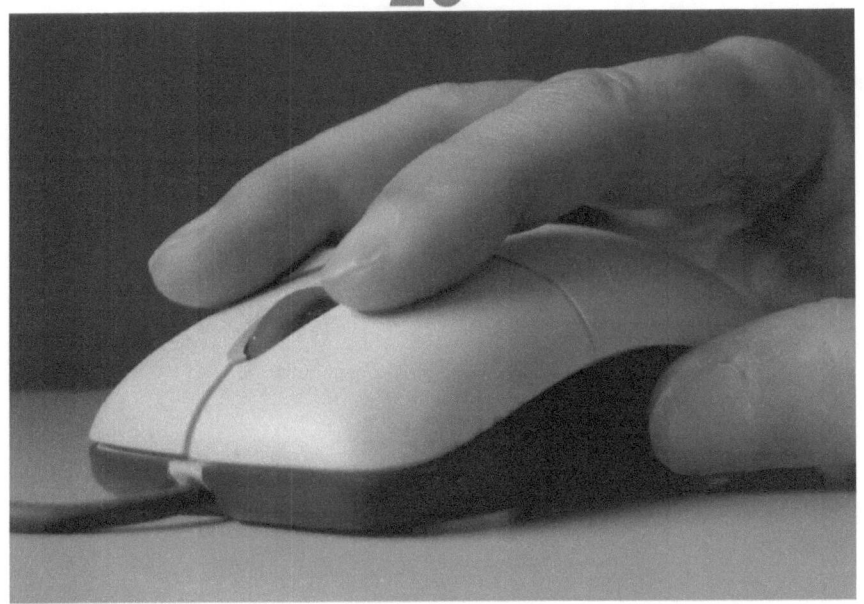

Demand Studios

Join a community of creative, talented contributors as a writer, copy editor or film maker. Demand Studios helps you work as much as you want, from wherever you want. Find consistent work and get paid weekly.

Website:
www.demandstudios.com

Sign Up/Registration Link:
https://www.demandstudios.com/application.html

Text Broker

Type your text and cash your check. Textbroker.com is your marketplace for unique and exclusive written articles created to your specifications.

Website:
www.Textbroker.com

Sign Up/Registration Link:
https://www.textbroker.com/en/author-signup.php

Image: Rasmus Thomsen/FreeDigitalPhotos.net

Voices

Use your unique speaking voice to earn income. Voices.com connects voice over talent to voice over talent seekers. Guest membership allows you go compete for work.
TIP: Practice your vocal craft with free digital audio software Audacity (www.audacity.sourceforge.net).

Website:
www.Voices.com

Sign Up/Registration Link:
http://www.voices.com/signup/guest

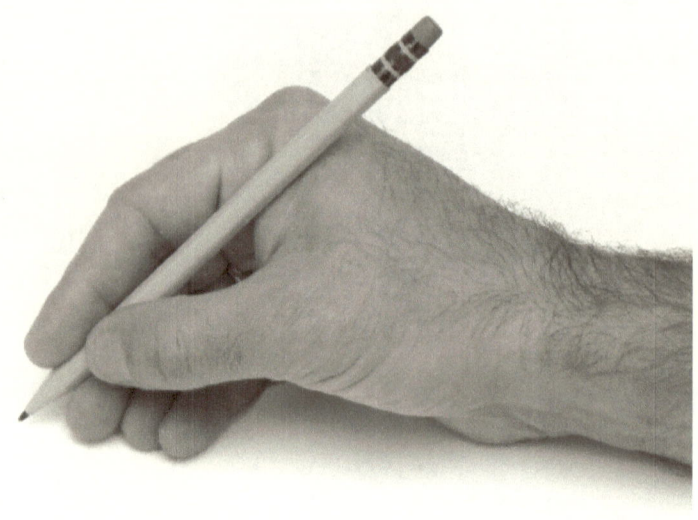

The Hollins Critic

Pen your poetry for pay. The Hollins Critic pays
$25.00 per poem, upon publication. All rights revert
to the author following publication. The Hollins Critic
reads poetry submissions from September 1 to
December 15 each year.

Website:
www.hollins.edu/grad/eng_writing/critic/critic.htm

Sign Up/Registration Link:
http://www.hollinscriticsubmissions.com/

Virtual Event Planning

Offer your services as a virtual event planner. Use MyPunchBowl.com to help you with planning, e-invitations, guest lists, and more. Since services are virtual, you could offer your event planning skills at a fraction of the cost of traditional event planners.

Website:
www.MyPunchBowl.com

Sign Up/Registration Link:
http://www.mypunchbowl.com/signup

Image: FreeDigitalPhotos.net

Ehomework Help

Tutor live via internet for pay. EhomeworkHelp.com pays between $10 - $75 per hour for their tutoring service.

Website:
www.EhomeworkHelp.com

Sign Up/Registration Link:
http://www.ehomeworkhelp.com/tutors/tutorapp.cfm

Image: Andy Newson/FreeDigitalPhotos.net

Word Zone

Speak another lingua franca to generate income. Word Zone.com offers online translation services and needs your help translating.

Website:
www.WordZone.com

Sign Up/Registration Link:
http://www.wordzone.com/firstvisit.shtml

Image: Simon Howden/FreeDigitalPhotos.net

ifreelance

Connect with businesses as a freelance professional to bid on projects and earn money doing what you love to do. ifreelance.com is a portal for your talents: from artists and graphic designers to programmers and writers.

Website:
www.ifreelance.com

Sign Up/Registration Link:
http://www.snip2.com/re/ifreelance

Image: Salvatore Vuono/FreeDigitalPhotos.net

Debt Shield

Get paid to refer leads for people seeking to settle their credit card debt and resolve their financial problems. Debtshield Inc. helps consumers avoid bankruptcy by providing a service for both debtors and creditors.

Website:
www.debtshield.com/affiliate/

Sign Up/Registration Link:
http://www.snip2.com/re/debtshield

Image: Graeme Weatherston FreeDigitalPhotos.net

ODesk

Start your freelance career at Odesk.com. Browse from thousands of companies hiring engineers, web designers, programmers, office assistants and more.

Website:
www.odesk.com

Sign Up/Registration Link:
https://www.odesk.com/w/signup.php

Image: Simon Howden, Suat Eman/FreeDigitalPhotos.net

Half.com

Check your closets and garage for treasures that other folks may want to buy. Post your prize possession on Half.com for others to see and purchase. No start-up or listing fees....Half.com only makes money when you do.

Website:
www.Half.com

Sign Up/Registration Link:
http://www.snip2.com/re/half

Image: FreeDigitalPhotos.net

Info Barrel

Make money contributing your expertise on a subject
with InfoBarrel.com. InfoBarrel is a revenue sharing
site that accepts articles from content contributors
who may write how-to guides, product reviews,
DIY guides and general information articles
called barrels.

Website:
www.InfoBarrel.com

Sign Up/Registration Link:
http://www.infobarrel.com/signup.php

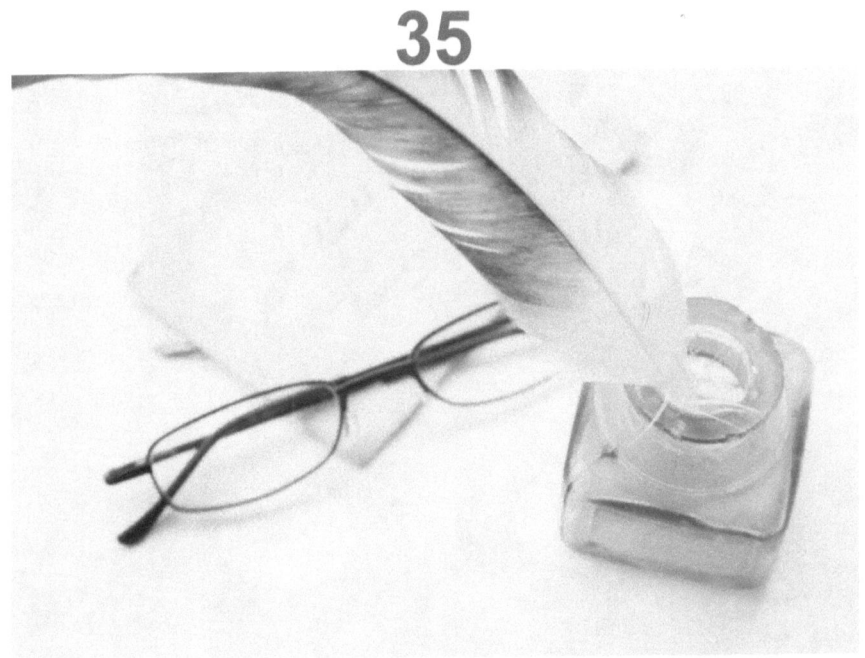

Image: Simon Howden/FreeDigitalPhotos.net

New England Review

Use your writing ability and earn. New England Review publishes quality fiction, poetry, and nonfiction that is both challenging and inviting to the general reader for $10 per page. Pays upon publication. Submissions period is September 1 through May 31 of each year.

Website:
www.nereview.com

Sign Up/Registration Link:
http://www.nereview.com/guidelines.html

Collectors Frenzy

Dust off your old LPs and earn some cash. Want to sell your inheritance of granny's old records but are unsure of the value? Find out previous final auction prices at CollectorsFrenzy.com and sell your records accordingly on Half.com

TIP: Go to www.vinylrecords.ch/Vinyl/vin_grading.htm for clues on how to grade the condition of records.

Website:
www.CollectorsFrenzy.com

Sign Up/Registration Link:
www.CollectorsFrenzy.com

Image: Simon Howden / FreeDigitalPhotos.net

HistoryNet

Marshal your knowledge of military history and earn income. HistoryNet.com publishes a military history magazine and pays freelance writers $300-$2,000 (depending on article/experience). Pays on publication.

Website:
www.historynet.com/magazines/military_history

Sign Up/Registration Info:
Send an email for specific guidelines and submission requirements to:
militaryhistory@weiderhistorygroup.com

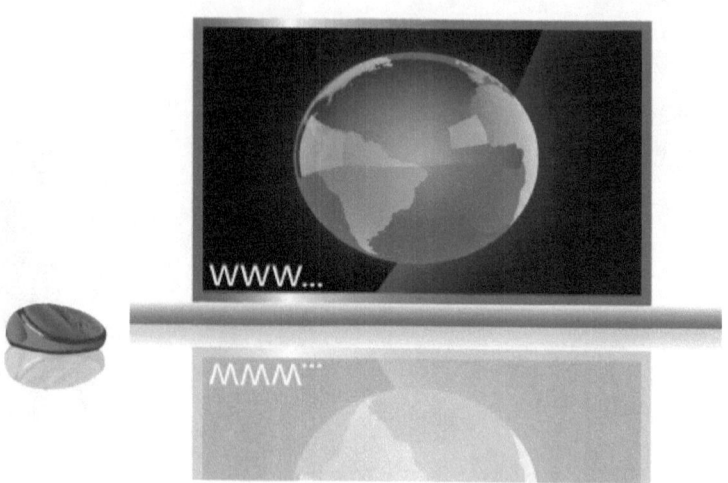

Rentacoder

Earn cash with your high tech coding skills. Once you register for free on Rentacoder.com, you'll receive daily bid requests from their registered buyers seeking your know-how in programming.

Website:
www.rentacoder.com

Sign Up/Registration Link:
http://www.snip2.com/re/rentacoder

Image: djcodrin/FreeDigitalPhotos.net

Freelance Designers

Draw upon your graphic design know-how and to earn extra income. Freelancelandesigners.com is a portal site where buyers can post projects and design freelancers can bid on them.

Website:
www.freelancedesigners.com

Sign Up/Registration Link:
http://www.freelancedesigners.com/register.cfm

Image: Simon Howden/FreeDigitalPhotos.net

Suite101

Reach millions of readers around the world with your writing aptitude and at the same time publish for pay online. Suite101.com is the place for freelance writers to showcase their work on just about any subject.

Website:
www.Suite101.com

Sign Up/Registration Link:
http://www.snip2.com/re/suite101

Image: djcodrin/FreeDigitalPhotos.net

Sell Your Hair

Grow luxurious locks, then lop off the length once you have a buyer who viewed yours tresses at TheHairTrader.com. Have a bidding war amongst wig designers or charge your price out right.

Website:
www.TheHairTrader.com

Sign Up/Registration Link:
http://thehairtrader.com/register.htm

Review Stream

Earn some cash just for writing reviews about the products you used or the stores you visited or cities you've seen. You could review anything around you and ReviewStream.com will pay you for all of the reviews.

Website:
www.ReviewStream.com

Sign Up/Registration Link:
http://dailydoc.com/writereviews.php

Get Paid for Data Entry

Get paid for your data entry skills. This is an aggregate listing of companies that pay for at home data entry positions.

Website:
www.GirlGetPaid.com

Sign Up/Registration Link:
http://girlgetpaid.com/category/data-entry-jobs

American Consumer Opinion

Post Share your opinions and earn money. American Consumer Opinion searches for a worldwide network of people who get paid for sharing their opinions and ideas by answering online surveys.

Website:
www.acop.com

Sign Up/Registration Link:
http://www.snip2.com/re/acop

45

Image: Maggie Smith/FreeDigitalPhotos.net

eHow

Craft popular articles for money. eHow.com is a site that will pay writers for content. The amount paid is based on the popularity of the article.

Website:
www.eHow.com

Sign Up/Registration Link:
https://forms.ehow.com/register.aspx

Image: Danilo Rizzuti/FreeDigitalPhotos.net

Mechanical Turk

Work on simple small jobs that people need completed for cash. Mechanical Turk lets scroll through task postings (called HITs) and you pick which ones you want to work on. The work is extremely simple like commenting on blogs, labeling images, rewriting sentences or paragraphs, writing short articles, and other quick work.

Website:
www.mturk.com/mturk/welcome

Sign Up/Registration Link:
http://www.snip2.com/re/aturk

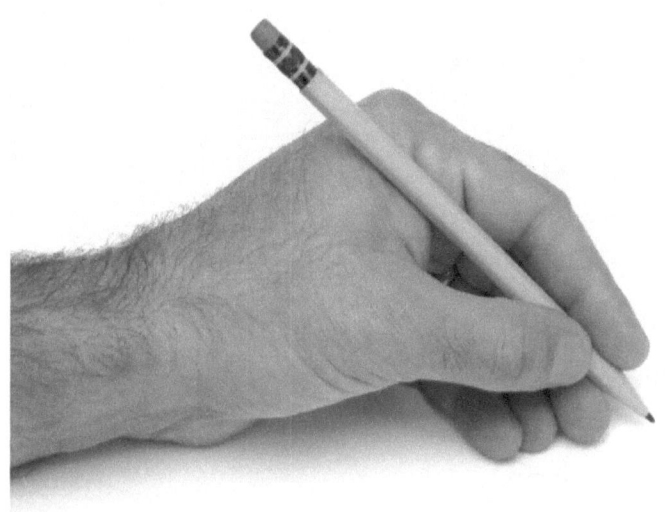

Image: Suat Eman/FreeDigitalPhotos.net

Xomba

Share information and earn with Xomba.
Xomba.com is an online community where you can
write, share, and comment to earn money. Xomba
uses adwords advertising to generate income to you.

Website:
www.Xomba.com

Sign Up/Registration Link:
http://www.snip2.com/re/xomba

Image: Francesco Marino/FreeDigitalPhotos.net

Scriptlance

Use your software programming, web development, content writing, graphic design and internet marketing abilities to bid on jobs. Scriptlance.com is a site matching freelancers and those seeking their skills.

Website:
www.scriptlance.com

Sign Up/Registration Link:
http://www.snip2.com/re/scriptlance

Image: Suat Eman/FreeDigitalPhotos.net

Sell Us Your Lamps

Change your lamps and get some extra cash. That ugly or not-so-ugly lamp that no longer suits your taste can be worth something to vintage lamp retailers. Check out tomsvintagelight.com *or* artdecolamps.com

Websites:
www.tomsvintagelight.com *or*
www.artdecolamps.com

Sign Up/Registration Link:
http://tomsvintagelighting.com/buy.html *or*

http://www.artdecolamps.com/sell-us-your-lamps

Image: Salvatore Vuono/FreeDigitalPhotos.net

Get Paid Blogging

Get paid to Blog. This is an aggregate listing of companies that offer blogging jobs.

Website:
www.GirlGetPaid.com

Sign Up/Registration Link:
http://girlgetpaid.com/category/blogger-jobs

Image: FreeDigitalPhotos.net

Focus Forward Online

Complete email surveys for cash or opportunities to win prizes. Very limited demographic information is required.
Typical compensation range: $1.00-$5.00 per survey.
Enrollment Survey Time: 1 minute

Website:
www.focusfwdonline.com

Sign Up/Registration Link:
http://www.snip2.com/re/forwardfocus

Image: Andy Newson/FreeDigitalPhotos.net

Go Freelance

Market your freelance services and find jobs to make money. GoFreelance.com provides a gateway to buyers needing a wide range of services: administrative, programming, graphic design, writing, etc.

Website:
www.GoFreelance.com

Sign Up/Registration Link:
http://www.gofreelance.com/join/comfort1/order.html